UPTON SINCLAIR'S
HE JUNGL
ADAPTED BY PETER KUPER

Dedicated to
The Workingmen of America
-Upton Sinclair
...and the Women too.
-P.K.

ISBN 1-56163-404-2, clothbound
ISBN 1-56163-411-5, paperback
The Jungle adapted by Peter Kuper
© 1991 First Publishing Inc.
All rights reserved
Book Design by Peter Kuper
Printed in China
3   2

Library of Congress Cataloging-in-Publication Data

Kuper, Peter, 1958-
    The jungle / Upton Sinclair ; adapted by Peter Kuper ; co-writer, Emily Russell.
       p. cm.
    ISBN 1-56163-402-2 (alk. paper) -- ISBN 1-56163-411-5 (pbk. : alk. paper)
    I. Russell, Emily. II. Sinclair, Upton, 1878-1968. Jungle. III. Title.

PN6727.K67J86 2004
741.5'973--dc22

2004053095

ComicsLit is an imprint
and trademark of

NANTIER · BEALL · MINOUSTCHINE
Publishing inc.
new york

IT WAS FOUR O'CLOCK WHEN THE CEREMONY WAS OVER...

THE PLACE WAS THE REAR ROOM OF A SALOON IN THAT PART OF CHICAGO KNOWN AS THE "BACK OF THE YARDS." THIS WAS THE SCENE OF THE WEDDING FEAST AND THE JOYFUL TRANSFIGURATION OF LITTLE ONA LUKOSZAITE, WHO HAD JUST BEEN MARRIED TO JURGIS RUDKUS!

JURGIS CAN TAKE UP A TWO-HUNDRED-AND-FIFTY-POUND QUARTER OF BEEF AND CARRY IT WITHOUT A STAGGER. AND NOW HE IS AS FRIGHTENED AS A HUNTED ANIMAL.

ONA IS NOT QUITE SIXTEEN. SHE FLUSHES RED WHEN SHE SEES THAT JURGIS IS WATCHING HER.

HER COUSIN, MARIJA, IS SCOLDING AND EXHORTING EVERYONE WITH HER TREMENDOUS VOICE.

ONA'S BROTHER, STANISLOVAS, KEEPS RUNNING UP BEHIND HER, WHISPERING, BREATHLESS.

JURGIS'S FATHER, OLD DEDE ANTANAS, GIVES A SPEECH. ONCE HE WAS A SCHOLAR AND MADE UP ALL THE LOVE LETTERS OF HIS FRIENDS.

TAMOSZIUS PLAYS LIKE ONE POSSESSED BY DEMONS. YOU CAN FEEL THEM IN THE AIR AROUND HIM.

THIS MUSIC IS THE MUSIC OF HOME. CHICAGO AND ITS FACTORIES AND ITS SLUMS FADE AWAY. JURGIS AND HIS FATHER AND AS MANY ANCESTORS BACK AS LEGEND COULD GO, HAD LIVED IN THAT PART OF LITHUANIA KNOWN AS THE IMPERIAL FOREST.

THE NEXT DAY THEY SALLIED FORTH. THEY HEARD THE CATTLE, A SOUND AS OF A FAR-OFF OCEAN CALLING. THE MEN IN THE KILLING BEDS OF PACKINGTOWN WORKED WITH FURIOUS INTENSITY, LITERALLY UPON THE RUN. IT WAS THE GREATEST GATHERING OF LABOR AND CAPITAL EVER IN ONE PLACE. IT SENT ITS PRODUCTS TO EVERY COUNTRY IN THE CIVILIZED WORLD, AND IT FURNISHED THE FOOD FOR NO LESS THAN THIRTY MILLION PEOPLE!

SPEAK ENGLISH?

NO.

SEE DOOR? TOMORROW. SEVEN O'CLOCK. UNDERSTAND?

NOW THE DREADFUL WINTER WAS UPON THEM.

ONA HAD FOUND A JOB SEWING COVERS ON HAMS.

STANISLOVAS STOOD HOUR AFTER HOUR AT A LARDING MACHINE, MAKING NEVER A MOTION AND THINKING NEVER A THOUGHT, SAVE FOR THE SETTING OF LARD CANS.

DEDE'S COUGH GREW WORSE EVERY DAY. HE CLUNG TO THE IDEA THAT HE WOULD GET BETTER, AND GO BACK TO HIS JOB.

BUT AT LAST ONE MORNING...

AMEN.

YET THE GERM OF HOPE WAS NOT TO BE KEPT FROM SPROUTING. TAMOSZIUS HAD GOTTEN INTO THE HABIT OF VISITING MARIJA.

THERE WAS NO RESISTING THE MUSIC OF TAMOSZIUS.

ONE NIGHT HE FOUND THE COURAGE TO SPEAK HIS HEART.

MARRY ME.

LITTLE BY LITTLE, WITH EACH MEMBER WORKING, THE FAMILY GAINED A FIRST-HAND KNOWLEDGE OF THE GREAT MAJORITY OF PACKINGTOWN SWINDLES.

FOR INSTANCE, THERE WAS NEVER THE LEAST ATTENTION PAID TO WHAT WAS CUT UP FOR SAUSAGE. THERE WOULD BE MEAT STORED IN GREAT PILES IN ROOMS, AND THE WATER FROM LEAKY ROOFS WOULD DRIP OVER IT, AND THOUSANDS OF RATS WOULD RACE ABOUT ON IT. THE PACKERS WOULD PUT POISON BREAD OUT FOR THEM, THEY WOULD DIE, AND THEN RATS, BREAD; AND MEAT WOULD GO INTO THE HOPPERS TOGETHER.

JURGIS WAS NO LONGER PERPLEXED WHEN HE HEARD MEN TALK OF FIGHTING FOR THEIR RIGHTS. NOW HE RECEIVED THE UNION DELEGATE IN A FAR DIFFERENT SPIRIT.

THROUGH THE UNION JURGIS HEARD OF BUBBLY CREEK. IT WAS REALLY AN OPEN SEWER, CONTAINING ALL THE DRAINAGE FROM THE PACKINGHOUSES. HERE AND THERE THE GREASE HAD CAKED SOLID. AN INGENIOUS PACKER HAD BEGUN TO GATHER THE FILTH IN SCOWS AND MAKE LARD OUT OF IT.

JURGIS MADE SURE EVERY MEMBER OF HIS FAMILY HAD UNION CARDS. HE NEVER MISSED A MEETING, NOR DID MARIJA. SHE, TOO, HAD HEARD STORIES...

A BUTCHER WHERE SHE WORKED WOULD DESCRIBE DISEASED CATTLE COVERED WITH BOILS. STUFF SUCH AS THIS MADE CANNED BEEF.

THEN THERE WERE THE VARIOUS AFFLICTIONS OF THE WORKERS. WORST OF ALL WERE THOSE WHO SERVED IN THE COOKING ROOMS. THEY OFTEN FELL INTO THE VATS, SOMETIMES BEING OVERLOOKED FOR DAYS, UNTIL ALL BUT THE BONES OF THEM HAD GONE OUT TO THE WORLD AS DURHAM'S PURE LEAF LARD!

THE UNION MADE A GREAT DIFFERENCE WITH JURGIS. HE ENROLLED IN A NIGHT SCHOOL TO LEARN ENGLISH. HE BECAME A CITIZEN AND LEARNED HOW TO MARK A BALLOT.

CHILL WINDS BEGAN TO WARN THEM THAT THE WINTER WAS COMING ON AGAIN.

THE WINTER WAS A TIME OF PERIL. WHEN A STEER BROKE LOOSE THE ROOM WOULD BE SO FULL OF STEAM THAT YOU COULD NOT MAKE ANYTHING OUT. IT WAS IN ONE OF THESE MELEES THAT JURGIS TWISTED HIS ANKLE...

HE GOT HOME SOMEHOW, SCARCELY ABLE TO SEE FOR THE PAIN.

HOUR AFTER HOUR, UNABLE TO WORK, THERE CAME TO HIM EMOTIONS THAT HE HAD NEVER KNOWN BEFORE, AS IF HE WERE STALKED BY A GRISLY PHANTOM. IT MIGHT BE TRUE AFTER ALL, WHAT OTHERS HAD TOLD HIM ABOUT LIFE, THAT THE BEST POWERS OF A MAN MIGHT NOT BE EQUAL TO IT.

THE ONE CONSOLATION OF HIS LONG IMPRISONMENT WAS THAT HE NOW HAD TIME TO PLAY WITH ANTANAS.

ONA WAS GETTING PALER EVERY DAY, AND IT PAINED HER THAT JURGIS DID NOT NOTICE.

THEY WERE IN FOR A SIEGE, THAT WAS PLAINLY TO BE SEEN...

13

AT LAST, IN THE SPRING, JURGIS LACED A BANDAGE ABOUT HIS ANKLE AND RETURNED TO WORK.

WE GAVE YOUR JOB TO SOMEONE ELSE.

HE TOOK HIS PLACE WITH THE MOB OF THE UNEMPLOYED.

WE'LL TAKE YOU.

THEY WOULD STAND AROUND EACH MORNING UNTIL RUN OFF.

MOVE ON!

HE WAS SECOND-HAND, A DAMAGED ARTICLE.

THEY HAD WORN HIM OUT, AND NOW THEY HAD THROWN HIM AWAY!

THERE IS A PLACE THAT WAITS FOR THE LOWEST MAN...

...THE FERTILIZER PLANT. HERE THEY WORKED WHERE THE DAYLIGHT NEVER CAME. THEY MADE FOUL-SMELLING THINGS INTO THINGS STILL MORE FOUL-SMELLING. THE MEN WOULD TALK ABOUT IT IN AWE-STRICKEN WHISPERS.

JURGIS ALMOST HOPED THERE WOULD BE NO OPENINGS. SOME THINGS WERE EVEN WORSE THAN STARVING TO DEATH.

HERE. TAKE THIS.

THE FERTILIZER SOAKED THROUGH EVERY PORE OF HIS SKIN. THERE WAS A FRIGHTFUL PAIN IN THE TOP OF HIS SKULL. STILL, WITH THE MEMORY OF HIS FOUR MONTHS' SIEGE BEHIND HIM, HE FOUGHT ON.

AT THE END OF THE DAY HE COULD SCARCELY STAND.

HE SMELLED SO THAT HE MADE THE WHOLE FAMILY ILL.

ONA WAS PREGNANT AGAIN. BUT THEY RARELY SPOKE OF IT. THEIR MOODS SO SELDOM CAME TOGETHER NOW.

HE WAS WORKING IN THE STEAMING PIT OF HELL, DAY AFTER DAY. BUT FROM THE UNENDING HORROR OF THAT THERE WAS A RESPITE...

JURGIS DISCOVERED DRINK.

ONA BEGAN TO FEEL THAT THERE WAS NO DELIVERANCE FOR THEM, NO HOPE.

IT SEEMED TO HIM THAT SHE HAD THE LOOK OF A HUNTED ANIMAL.

EVERY MILE THAT HE GOT FROM PACKINGTOWN MEANT ANOTHER LOAD FROM HIS MIND.

IN THE FALL JURGIS BID FAREWELL TO THE COUNTRY. ALL THE JOY WENT OUT OF TRAMPING WITH THE ONSET OF WINTER. HE SET OUT FOR CHICAGO AGAIN.

WILLING TO WORK UNDERGROUND-- DIGGING RAILROAD TUNNELS?

SURE.

THERE WOULD BE FALLING ROCKS AND CRUSHED SUPPORTS AND PREMATURE EXPLOSIONS.

HE BEGAN THE LONG WEARY ROUND OF FACTORIES AND WAREHOUSES.

SO IT WAS THAT ONE DAY...

CLANG CLANG CLANG

WHEN HE OPENED HIS EYES AGAIN HE WAS LYING IN THE COUNTY HOSPITAL.

30

SUDDENLY, AS BY THE GIFT OF A MAGIC KEY, HE HAD ENTERED INTO A WORLD WHERE MONEY AND ALL THE GOOD THINGS OF LIFE CAME FREELY. ONE NIGHT JACK INTRODUCED HIM TO MIKE SCULLY, THE DEMOCRATIC BOSS OF THE STOCKYARDS.

WITH ELECTIONS COMING UP, I COULD USE A MAN LIKE YOU IN PACKING-TOWN.

I'M BLACK-LISTED.

LET ME WORRY ABOUT THAT.

JURGIS CAME TO UNDERSTAND THE INS AND OUTS OF THE POLITICAL GAME. HE WENT FROM MAN TO MAN. THIS YEAR THE DEMOCRATS WERE PAYING FOUR DOLLARS A VOTE, THE REPUBLICANS ONLY THREE.

HE HAD NO IDEA THAT IT WAS SCULLY WHO WAS TO BLAME FOR THE UNPAVED STREET IN WHICH LITTLE ANTANAS HAD DROWNED, SCULLY WHO WAS AN OWNER OF THE COMPANY WHICH HAD TURNED HIS FAMILY OUT OF THEIR HOUSE.

TO HIM, SCULLY WAS THE BIGGEST MAN HE HAD EVER MET. HE COULD NOT GRASP THAT SCULLY WAS BUT A TOOL AND PUPPET OF THE PACKERS.

THAT MAY, THE CONTRACT BETWEEN THE PACKERS AND THE UNIONS EXPIRED. AN AGREEMENT COULD NOT BE REACHED. THE GREAT "BEEF STRIKE" WAS ON.

THE PACKERS NEED MEN RIGHT NOW.

YOU MEAN CROSS THE PICKET LINE AND WORK AS A SCAB?

BUT JURGIS DID AS HE WAS TOLD.

THE PACKERS BROUGHT IN MEN FROM THE DEEP SOUTH, PROMISING THEM FIVE DOLLARS A DAY AND BOARD--AND BEING CAREFUL NOT TO MENTION THERE WAS A STRIKE.

JURGIS WAS SOON GIVEN A PROMOTION. AT LAST, HE WAS TO BE A BOSS!

HE GOT USED TO IT QUICKLY ENOUGH. HE STORMED AND CURSED AND DROVE THE MEN UNTIL THEY WERE READY TO DROP.

ONE DAY SOME CATTLE ESCAPED FROM THE YARDS. JURGIS AND HIS GANG WERE SENT OUTSIDE TO BRING BACK THE ANIMALS. BUT THE STRIKERS HAD GOTTEN HOLD OF THEM.

RIOT!

THE STRIKERS WERE OUTNUMBERED. THEY COULD NOT WIN THIS BATTLE, BUT THEY WOULD PUT UP A FIGHT. THE DREAM OF RESISTANCE HAUNTS A PERSON, HOPE CONTENDING WITH FEAR, UNTIL SUDDENLY A FETTER SNAPS--THE DREAM BECOMES AN ACT!

42

JURGIS COULD NOT GET OVER THE SHOCK OF ALL THAT MARIJA HAD TOLD HIM.

MEMORIES STIRRED THAT HAD BEEN SLEEPING SO LONG HE HAD COUNTED THEM DEAD. IT HAD BEEN THE TASK OF HIS RECENT LIFE TO FIGHT THEM DOWN, BUT NOW THEY OVERWHELMED HIM.

HE THOUGHT OF ANTANAS, WHOM HE HAD MEANT TO MAKE A MAN. HE THOUGHT OF HIS FATHER, WHO HAD BLESSED THEM ALL. HE THOUGHT OF ONA AND THEIR LOVE.

HIS OLD GHOSTS BECKONED TO HIM. HE HEARD THE OLD VOICES OF HIS SOUL.

RAAAH....

43

ANOTHER RALLY. REMEMBERING HIS TREATMENT OF THE NIGHT BEFORE, HE HESITATED. BUT IT WAS SO COLD OUTSIDE...

RAAAH...

TRY AS HE MIGHT TO STAY AWAKE...

HE SAT UP WITH A START, EXPECTING TO SEE A POLICEMAN.

IF YOU TRY TO LISTEN, YOU MIGHT FIND YOU'RE INTERESTED.

THE SPEAKER'S VOICE WAS VIBRANT WITH EMOTION.

SUDDENLY IT SEEMED TO HIM THAT THE MAN WAS SPEAKING DIRECTLY TO HIM.

...I HAVE BEEN IN YOUR PLACE. I HAVE KNOWN WHAT IT IS TO LIVE UPON A CRUST OF BREAD AND SLEEP IN STAIRWAYS...

It was as though the sky split above him. Even if he were to suffer as he had before, he would no longer be the sport of circumstance. He would be a man, with a will and a purpose.

The thing to do was not to talk, but to do.

Like a single sound there came a cry from a thousand people.

CHICAGO WILL BE OURS!

CHICAGO WILL BE OURS!

CHICAGO WILL BE OURS!

Upton Sinclair was born in Baltimore in 1878 and was raised in poverty. His life as a writer began when he was 15 with the dime novels he turned out to pay his way through the College of the City of New York. He progressed to more mainstream fiction and produced six novels while enrolled as a graduate at Columbia, among them *King Midas* (1901) and *Manassas* (1904). These early works were not well received by the book-buying public and Sinclair earned very little from them; it took the publication of *The Jungle* in 1906 to assure his literary and commercial success. Perceived as a muckraking expose of the meat-packing industry, *The Jungle* was in fact written to advocate socialism. Sinclair, who had become a socialist in early life, used his royalties from the book to found the Helicon Home Colony, a prototypical socialist cooperative in Englewood, New Jersey; the experiment was abandoned after a mysterious fire in 1907. In 1915, Sinclair moved to California, where he unsuccessfully ran for governor four times, coming closest to election in 1938 when he forged the state's progressive elements into the EPIC (End Poverty in California) coalition. The campaign was acrimonious - his opponent was backed by the entrenched business community - and Sinclair was narrowly defeated. His activism was also expressed in such books as *The Metropolis* (1907), about morality in a society controlled by wealth; *The Profits of Religion* (1918), which espouses the viewpoint that organized religion is a capitalist tool for keeping the masses in their place; and *Boston* (1928), based on the executions of the anarchists Sacco and Vanzetti. In 1940 Sinclair published *World's End*, the first in a series of 11 novels starring the character Lanny Buddand covering international politics from 1913 to the height of the Cold War in 1953; one of the books in the series *Dragon's Teeth* (1942), was awarded the Pulitzer Prize. In addition to novels, Sinclair wrote short stories, plays and pamphlets, and has over 100 works to his credit. He continued to write into his eighties; the novel *It Happened to Didymus* was published in 1958, and his autobiography appeared in 1962. He died in 1968.

Peter Kuper was born in 1958 and grew up in Cleveland, Ohio. He moved to New York in 1977 and attended Pratt Institute. In 1979 he co-founded *World War 3 Illustrated*, a political zine, and remains on the editorial board to this day. He has taught courses in comics at the School of Visual Arts in New York City since 1986 and since 1988 has co-art directed *INX*, an editorial illustration group syndicated through the web at www.inxart.com. His illustrations appear in magazines and newspapers around the world including Time and The New York Times as well as Mad where he has drawn *Spy vs. Spy* every month since 1997.
He has written and illustrated numerous graphic novels including *The System, Stripped, Comics Trips, Eye of the Beholder, Mind's Eye, Speechless* and *Sticks and Stones*. His other adaptations include Franz Kafka's *The Metamorphosis* as well as *Give It Up!* collecting nine Kafka short stories. More of his work can be seen at www.peterkuper.com.

Peter wishes to acknowledge a number of people who made this adaptation possible. First and foremost, Emily Russell, whose tremendous efforts in co-adapting the text made this daunting process a pleasure, Wade Roberts for initially giving me the opportunity to do this project as well as a number of people at First Publishing for helping to see the book through all its stages, Ken Levin for being such a stand up guy, Terry Nantier and Martin Satryb for presenting it so beautifully, Tomm Scalera for stencil cutting, Willie Shubert for lettering and Ryan Inzana for production assistance. As always, thanks for the love and support of my wife, Betty and all of my friends and family. Finally, thanks to Upton Sinclair, whose work has been a guiding light--demonstrating so powerfully that art can be used as an instrument for change and benefit so many in the process.